NOV - - 2014

The Age of Dinosaurs

Meet Deinonychus

Written by Jayne Raymond

Illustrations by Leonello Calvetti and Luca Massini

Cavendish Square

New York

Published in 2015 by Cavendish Square Publishing, LLC
243 5th Avenue, Suite 136, New York, NY 10016

This publication represents the opinions and views of the author based on his or her personal experience, knowledge, and research. The information in this book serves as a general guide only. The author and publisher have used their best efforts in preparing this book and disclaim liability rising directly or indirectly from the use and application of this book.

CPSIA Compliance Information: Batch #WS14CSQ

All websites were available and accurate when this book was sent to press.

Library of Congress Cataloging-in-Publication Data

Raymond, Jayne, author.
Meet Deinonychus / Jayne Raymond.
pages cm. — (The age of dinosaurs)
Includes bibliographical references and index.
ISBN 978-1-62712-794-3 (hardcover) — ISBN 978-1-62712-795-0 (paperback) ISBN 978-1-62712-796-7 (ebook)
1. Deinonychus—Juvenile literature. I. Title.

QE862.S3R38 2015
567.912—dc23

2014001528

Editorial Director: Dean Miller
Copy Editor: Cynthia Roby
Art Director: Jeffrey Talbot
Designer: Douglas Brooks
Photo Researcher: J8 Media
Production Manager: Jennifer Ryder-Talbot
Production Editor: David McNamara
Illustrations by Leonello Calvetti and Luca Massini

The photographs in this book are used by permission and through the courtesy of:
BGSmith/Shutterstock.com, 8; Krzysztof Wiktor/Shutterstock.com, 8; Jay Boucher/Shutterstock.com, 8;
Jon Bilous/Shutterstock.com, 8; Didier Descouens/File:Deinonychus.png/Wikimedia Commons, 20;
KIKE CALVO VWPics/SuperStock, 21.

Printed in the United States of America

CONTENTS

Late Triassic	Early Jurassic	Middle Jurassic
227 – 206 million years ago.	206 –176 million years ago.	176 – 159 million years ago.

A CHANGING WORLD

The Earth has been home to many different kinds of creatures in its 4.6 billion-year history, but dinosaurs have to be among the most interesting.

The word "dinosaur" comes from two Greek words: *deinos*, meaning "terrible," and *sauros*, which means "lizard."

Understanding dinosaurs begins with learning about the geological history of the Earth. Our planet's history is divided into different lengths of time called eras, periods, epochs, and ages. The time when dinosaurs existed is called the Mezozoic era, which is divided into three periods: the Triassic, lasting 42 million years; Jurassic,

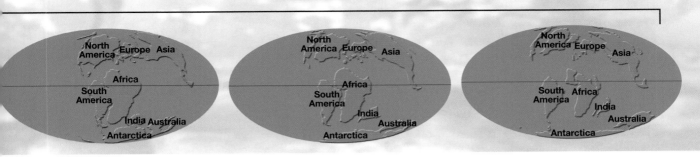

Late Jurassic	Early Cretaceous	Late Cretaceous
159 – 144 million years ago.	144 – 99 million years ago.	99 – 65 million years ago.

61 million years; and Cretaceous, 79 million years. Altogether, dinosaurs ruled the Earth for over 160 million years!

Dinosaurs died out 65 million years before humans first appeared on Earth. The world when the dinosaurs lived was very different from the one we know today. It was warmer, the continents were not in the same place, and grass did not even exist!

5

A TERRIFYING HUNTER

Deinonychus (pronounced dy-NON-i-kes) was a saurischian dinosaur belonging to the order of *Saurischia*, meaning "lizard-hipped," and the suborder *Theropoda*, meaning "beast-footed." It is a member of the *Dromaeosauridae* family, from the Latin for "running lizards." Only a single species of Deinonychus, translated to "terrible claw," is known: *Deinonychus antirrhopus*.

A carnivorous (meat-eating) dinosaur known for its intelligence, Deinonychus was bipedal, or walked on two legs, and shared a number of features common to birds. The dinosaur had unusually long arms and hands, and a wrist that was able to repeatedly bend sideways. Each of its three fingers was a well-developed claw. These features helped Deinonychus quickly attack and injure its prey.

The dinosaur's 70 sharp, inward-curved teeth made it easy to bite and chew flesh as well as keep smaller prey from escaping its jaws.

A small, agile, and quick-moving dinosaur, Deinonychus measured 8 to 10 feet (2.5 to 3.5 meters) long, tail included. It stood nearly 5 feet (1.5 meters) tall, weighed up to 175 pounds (80 kilograms), and its head measured just under one foot (30 centimeters) long.

FINDING DEINONYCHUS

Deinonychus roamed the western areas of North America, specifically Montana, Wyoming, and Oklahoma. This was during the Cretaceous period between 110 and 115 million years ago. Paleontologists also believe that the dinosaurs possibly lived in Maryland. Because Deinonychus was fairly small in a world of huge dinosaurs, it roamed and hunted in packs. Deinonychus preferred forest and green areas because that was where its prey, plant-eating dinosaurs, generally gathered in herds.

Montana

Wyoming

Oklahoma

Maryland

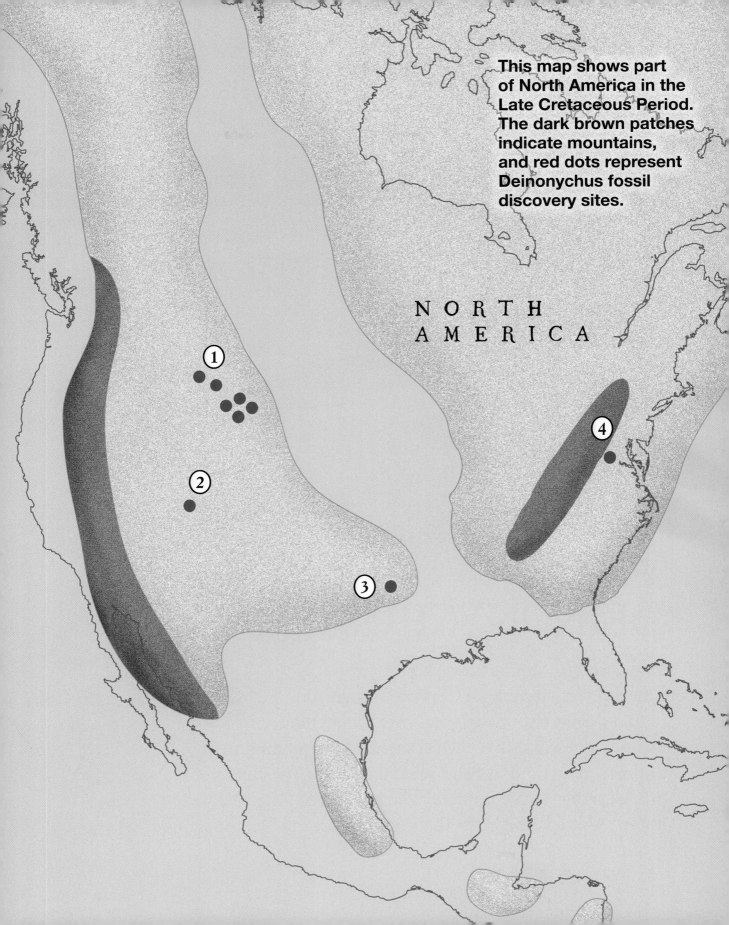

This map shows part of North America in the Late Cretaceous Period. The dark brown patches indicate mountains, and red dots represent Deinonychus fossil discovery sites.

NORTH AMERICA

YOUNG DEINONYCHUS

Deinonychus dug its nest into the mud. The rim was circular and raised. It formed a depression in the shape of a bowl. The female Deinonychus laid two eggs at once and a maximum of thirty each time. It took several days for the clutch, or nest of eggs, to complete. The eggs were long and had finely wrinkled shells. At the right time, baby Deinonychus broke out of the shells.

DEADLY TECHNIQUES

Deinonychus did not have many rivals when it came to hunting. The lightweight and bird-like structure of its body allowed Deinonychus to reach higher speeds than many other carnivorous dinosaurs. Paleontologists believe that Deinonychus hunted in packs. They would leap toward their prey with their clawed hands and strike swiftly. Their targets would quickly become defenseless. This gave Deinonychus a dangerous advantage at ambushing and trapping its much larger prey, which included sauropods, ornithopods, and the armored ankylosaurians. This predatory instinct was innate, or already present, in Deinonychus at birth.

A CLEVER DINOSAUR

Deinonychus is considered by paleontologists to have had a rather large brain—one greater in size than that of other dinosaurs. This does not prove that Deinonychus was the smartest among all dinosaurs, but it was a very intelligent animal.

Paleontologists are convinced that Deinonychus was very organized, specifically when hunting in packs. When the dinosaurs, for example, spotted the large Ankylosaurus, they needed to communicate with each other and make a plan to overpower the prey. This type of strategy required intelligence, teamwork, good coordination, and excellent eyesight to carry out.

MEALTIME

Deinonychus was a carnivore. Paleontologists suggest that the dinosaur may have preyed on large plant-eating dinosaurs. Fast moving and clever, Deinonychus was capable of jumping great distances. This made it an extremely deadly force against other dinosaurs when hunting them for food. The sickle-like claw in the hatchling's inner toe was probably already developed at birth. This allowed baby Deinonychus to capture its first prey: small animals such as lizards, salamanders, or primitive mammals similar to mice.

INSIDE DEINONYCHUS

Deinonychus's lightweight skull measured just over 16 inches (40.6 cm) in length. It had large openings for the dinosaur's eyes and the muscles that allowed its jaws to open and close. Its teeth were sharp like knives and curved. The dinosaur's hindfoot had four toes, but only three were well developed. The toe with the large claw was short and robust. Deinonychus's forefoot was large and had thin fingers with claws that were pointed and hooked.

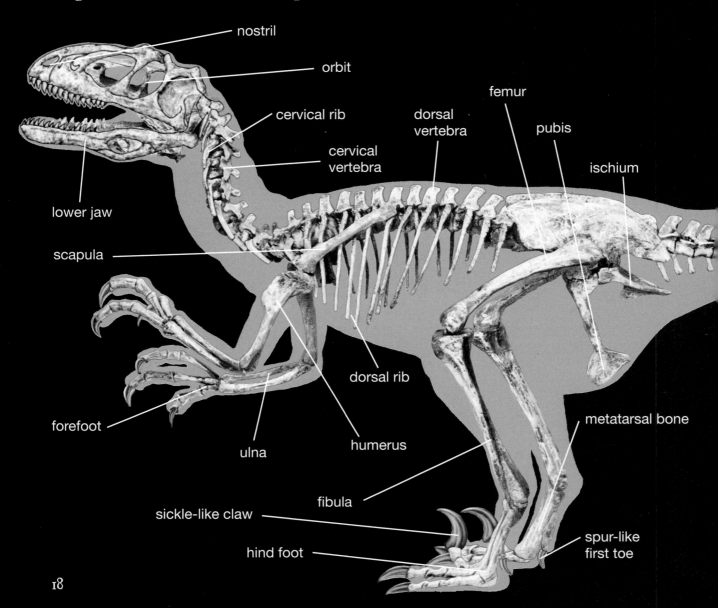

nostril

orbit

femur

cervical rib

dorsal
vertebra

pubis

cervical
vertebra

ischium

lower jaw

scapula

dorsal rib

forefoot

metatarsal bone

ulna

humerus

fibula

sickle-like claw

spur-like
first toe

hind foot

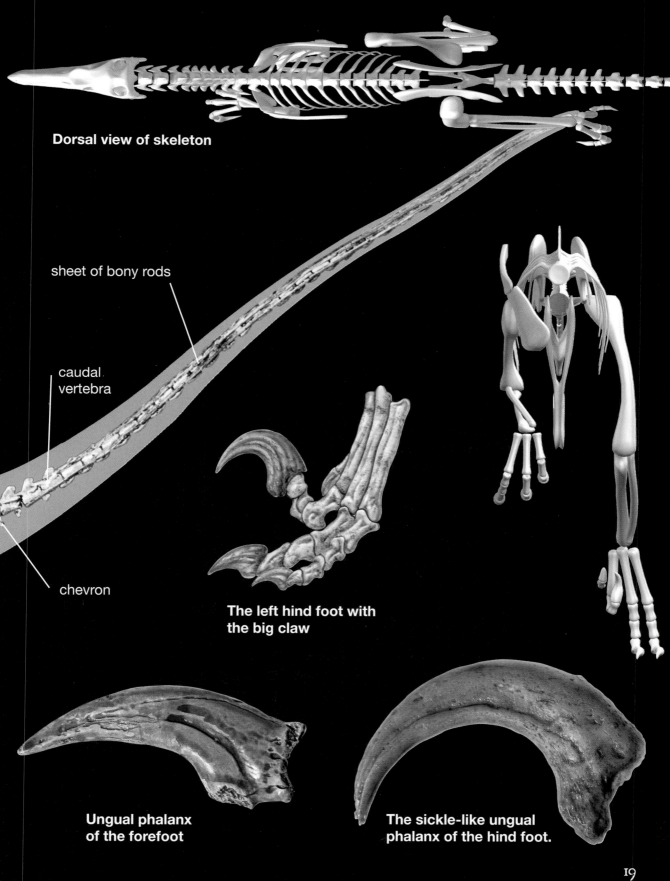

Dorsal view of skeleton

sheet of bony rods

caudal
vertebra

chevron

The left hind foot with
the big claw

**Ungual phalanx
of the forefoot**

**The sickle-like ungual
phalanx of the hind foot.**

UNEARTHING DEINONYCHUS

The first Deinonychus fossils were unearthed in 1964 by American paleontologists John Ostrom and Grant Meyer in the Bighorn Basin of southern Montana. In 1969, Ostrom named the fossil Deinonychus, Greek for "terrible claw," because of the large claw on its hind foot. When Ostrom further examined the fossil, he found that its forefeet were similar to those of birds. This discovery suggested the idea that birds are descended from dinosaurs. This is an accepted theory among paleontologists today.

A Deinonychus skull.

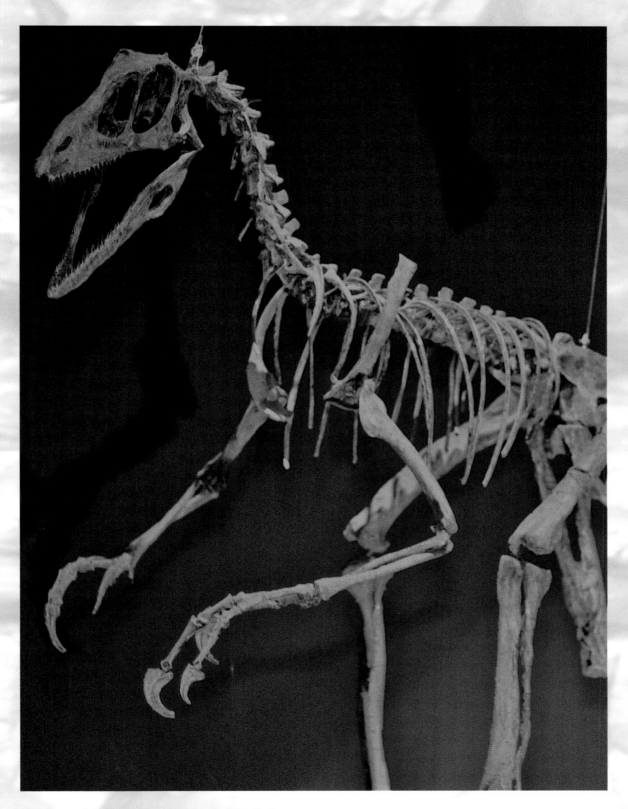

A complete Deinonychus skeleton.

THE DROMAEOSAURIDS

Discovery sites of the Dromaeosaurids are shown on these pages

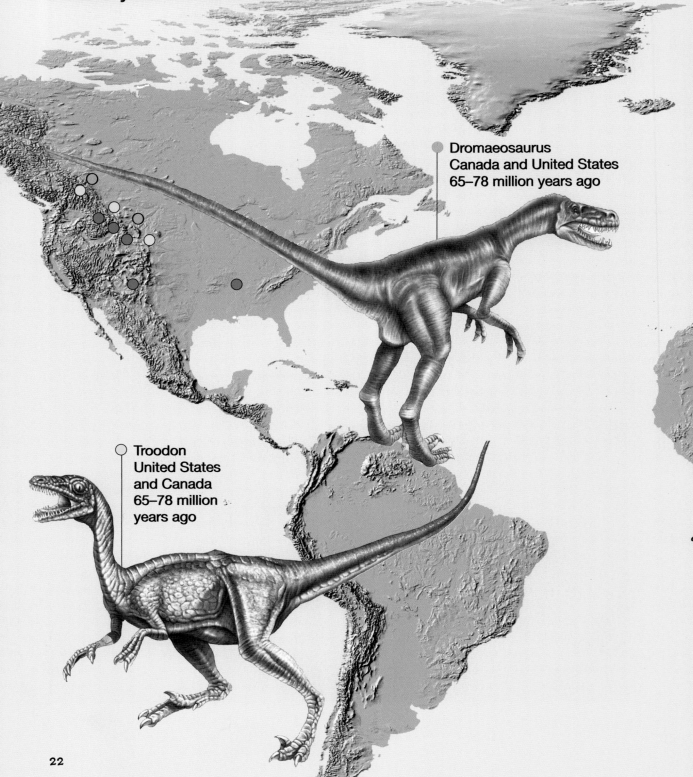

Dromaeosaurus
Canada and United States
65–78 million years ago

Troodon
United States
and Canada
65–78 million
years ago

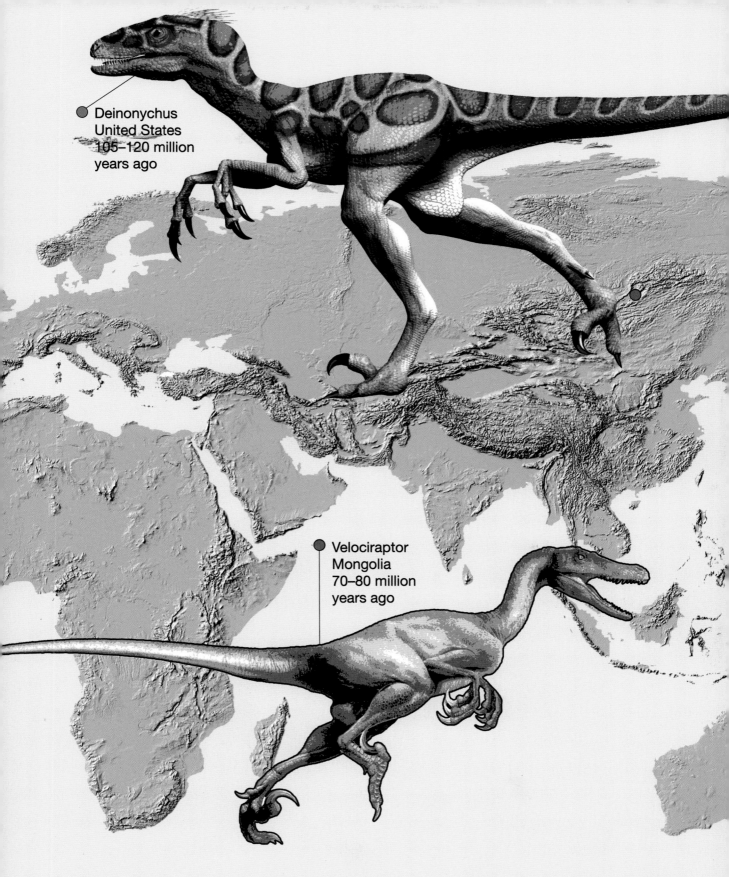

Deinonychus
United States
105–120 million
years ago

Velociraptor
Mongolia
70–80 million
years ago

THE GREAT EXTINCTION

What caused the dinosaurs to disappear? Scientists think that 65 million years ago—50 million years after the time of Deinonychus—the impact of a large meteorite hitting the Earth did the job. There was enough dust thrown into the air to block the sunlight for a long time. This caused the temperature to drop drastically, killing many plants.

A possible site for this meteor strike is a wide crater located on Mexico's coast. It was formed exactly 65 million years ago.

The plant-eating dinosaurs would have starved or frozen to death, leaving meat-eating dinosaurs without their food supply. Scientists believe dinosaurs did not die out completely, however, and that chickens and other birds are the descendants of the large creatures.

A DINOSAUR'S FAMILY TREE

The oldest dinosaur fossils are 220–225 million years old and have been found all over the world.

Dinosaurs are divided into two groups. Saurischians are similar to reptiles, with the pubic bone directed forward, while the Ornithischians are like birds, with the pubic bone directed backward.

Saurischians are subdivided in two main groups: Sauropodomorphs, to which quadrupeds and vegetarians belong; and Theropods, which include bipeds and predators.

Ornithischians are subdivided into three large groups: Thyreophorans, which include the quadrupeds Stegosaurians and Ankylosaurians; Ornithopods; and Marginocephalians, which are subdivided into the bipedal Pachycephalosaurians and the mainly quadrupedal Ceratopsians.

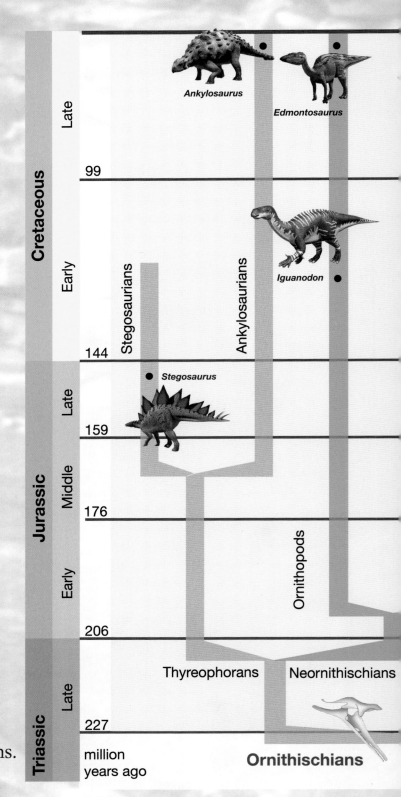

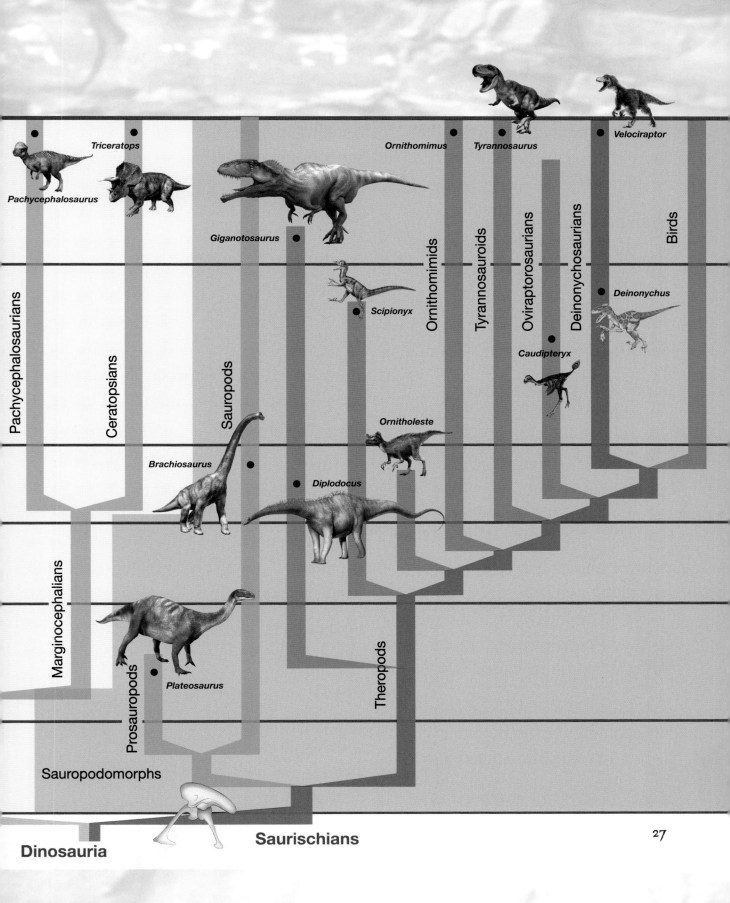

Pachycephalosaurus

● Triceratops

Giganotosaurus ●

Ornithomimus ●

Tyrannosaurus ●

Velociraptor ●

Ornithomimids

Tyrannosauroids

Oviraptorosaurians

Deinonychosaurians

Birds

● Scipionyx

● Deinonychus

Caudipteryx ●

Pachycephalosaurians

Ceratopsians

Sauropods

Ornitholeste

Brachiosaurus ●

● Diplodocus

Marginocephalians

Theropods

Prosauropods

● Plateosaurus

Sauropodomorphs

Dinosauria

Saurischians

27

A SHORT VOCABULARY OF DINOSAURS

Bipedal: pertaining to an animal moving on two feet alone, almost always those of the hind legs.

Bone: hard tissue made mainly of calcium phosphate; single element of the skeleton.

Carnivore: a meat-eating animal.

Caudal: pertaining to the tail.

Cenozoic Era (Caenozoic, Tertiary Era): the interval of geological time between 65 million years ago and present day.

Cervical: pertaining to the neck.

Claws: the fingers and toes of predator animals end with pointed and sharp nails, called claws. Those of plant-eaters end with blunt nails, called hooves.

Cretaceous Period: the interval of geological time between 144 and 65 million years ago.

Egg: a large cell enclosed in a porous shell produced by reptiles and birds to reproduce themselves.

Epoch: a memorable date or event.

Evolution: changes in the character states of organisms, species, and higher ranks through time.

Extinct: when something, such as a species of animal, is no longer existing.

Feathers: outgrowth of the skin of birds and some dinosaurs, used in flight and in providing insulation and protection for the body. They evolved from reptilian scales.

Forage: to wander in search of food.

Fossil: evidence of life in the past. Not only bones, but footprints and trails made by animals, as well as dung, eggs or plant resin, when fossilized, are fossils.

Herbivore: a plant-eating animal.

Jurassic Period: the interval of geological time between 206 and 144 million years ago.

Mesozoic Era (Mesozoic, Secondary Era): the interval of geological time between 248 and 65 million years ago.

Pack: a group of predator animals acting together to capture their prey.

Paleontologist: a scientist who studies and reconstructs the prehistoric life.

Paleozoic Era (Paleozoic, Primary Era): the interval of geological time between 570 and 248 million years ago.

Predator: an animal that preys on other animals for food.

Raptor (raptorial): a bird of prey, such as an eagle, hawk, falcon, or owl.

Rectrix (plural rectrices): any of the larger feathers in a bird's tail that are important in helping its flight direction.

Scavenger: an animal that eats dead animals.

Skeleton: a structure of an animal's body made of several different bones. One primary function is to protect delicate organs such as the brain, lungs, and heart.

Skin: the external, thin layer of the animal body. Skin cannot fossilize, unless it is covered by scales, feathers, or fur.

Skull: bones that protect the brain and the face.

Teeth: tough structures in the jaws used to hold, cut, and sometimes process food.

Terrestrial: living on land.

Triassic Period: the interval of geological time between 248 and 206 million years ago.

Unearth: to find something that was buried beneath the earth.

Vertebrae: the single bones of the backbone; they protect the spinal cord.

DINOSAUR WEBSITES

Dino Database
www.dinodatabase.com
Get the latest news on dinosaur research and discoveries.
This site is pretty advanced, so you may need help from a teacher
or parent to find what you're looking for.

Dinosaurs for Kids
www.kidsdinos.com
There's basic information about most dinosaur types, and you can
play dinosaur games, vote for your favorite dinosaur, and learn
about the study of dinosaurs, paleontology.

Dinosaur Train
pbskids.org/dinosaurtrain
From the PBS show *Dinosaur Train*, you can watch videos,
print out pages to color, play games, and learn lots of facts about
so many dinosaurs!

Discovery Channel Dinosaur Videos
discovery.com/video-topics/other/other-topics-dinosaur-videos.htm
Watch almost 100 videos about the life of dinosaurs!

The Natural History Museum
www.nhm.ac.uk/kids-only/dinosaurs
Take a quiz to see how much you know about dinosaurs—or a quiz
to tell you what type of dinosaur you'd be! There's also
a fun directory of dinosaurs, including some cool 3-D views of
your favorites.

MUSEUMS

American Museum of Natural History, New York, NY
www.amnh.org

Carnegie Museum of Natural History, Pittsburgh, PA
www.carnegiemnh.org

Denver Museum of Nature and Science, Denver, CO
www.dmns.org

Dinosaur National Monument, Dinosaur, CO
www.nps.gov/dino

The Field Museum, Chicago, IL
fieldmuseum.org

University of California Museum of Paleontology, Berkeley, CA
www.ucmp.berkeley.edu

Museum of the Rockies, Bozeman, MT
www.museumoftherockies.org

National Museum of Natural History, Smithsonian Institution,
Washington, DC
www.mnh.si.edu

Royal Tyrrell Museum of Palaeontology, Drumheller, Canada
www.tyrrellmuseum.com

Sam Noble Museum of Natural History, Norman, OK
www.snomnh.ou.edu

Yale Peabody Museum of Natural History, New Haven, CT
peabody.yale.edu

INDEX

Page numbers in **boldface** are illustrations.